COOKING WITHOUT BARRIERS
Recipes by Children for Every Hungry Child

This book belongs to

This book is dedicated to the hungry children around the world.
You are not alone.

Published by
Sun Behind The Cloud Publications Ltd
PO Box 15889, Birmingham, B16 6NZ

in association with

A World Without Barriers
Charity Registration Number: 291922

This edition first published in paperback 2016

Photography by Shellina Walji
shellina@waljis.co.uk

A CIP catalogue record for this book is available from the British Library

ISBN 978-1-908110-31-2
Printed in the United Kingdom

www.sunbehindthecloud.com

www.worldwithoutbarriers.org

In the Name of God, The Beneficent, The Merciful.

O God, be kind to me through the survival of my children,
Setting them right for me and allowing me to enjoy them.
My God, make long their lives for me, increase their terms,
Bring up the smallest for me, strengthen the weakest for me,
Make good for me their bodies, their religious dedication,
and their moral traits,
And everything that concerns me of their affair,
And pour out for me and upon my hand their provisions!
Make them pious, fearing, insightful, hearing, and obedient towards You,
and well-disposed toward Your friends…
…To All the faithful, please grant the like of what I have asked for myself
and my children,
In the immediate of this world, and the deferred of the next!
Surely You are the Near, the Responder, the All-hearing, the All-knowing…

Ali ibn Husayn, Zayn al-Abideen,
Sahifah Sajjadiyya, Dua No. 25

CONTENTS

Sweet

A WORLD WITHOUT BARRIERS (WWB) is a UK registered, independent, voluntary, non-profit and non-governmental organisation. Our intention is to help everyone on the basis of humanity, with the main focus being placed on helping orphans, the needy, the destitute, and the most vulnerable worldwide. Our aim is to bring the plight of the poor to you and to help change lives.

We do not differentiate on the grounds of faith, race, culture, tradition, or colour. In our view, we are all one people who share the same planet, a planet that if you were to observe from space, has no barriers, no borders, and whose resources are for everyone, hence the name 'A World Without Barriers.' We remain independent by staying away from all forms of politics and this helps us to work independently and sincerely.

OUR AIM IS TO HELP MANKIND BY
- Supporting orphans with financial, educational and medical assistance
- Providing education & training
- Assisting in the prevention or relief of poverty
- Economic/Community Development/Employment
- General Charitable Purposes

SOCIAL MEDIA
You can keep up to date with our activities on Social Media by visiting:
https://www.facebook.com/WorldWithoutBarriers/

www.worldwithoutbarriers.org
info@worldwithoutbarriers.org

All profits raised from this book will go towards feeding hungry children around the world.

WITH THE MONEY RAISED WE WILL FOCUS ON:

LOOKING AFTER ORPHANS
Orphans and destitute children in Iraq, Syria, Yemen, Afghanistan, Liberia, Morocco, Bangladesh, India, Pakistan, Senegal, Ethiopia, China, Burma, Comoros Island, United Kingdom and Worldwide.

EDUCATION WITHOUT BARRIERS
Feeding children for education in Liberia and in India. We have a scheme where we provide families with food items such as rice, lentils, oil, flour, spices, poultry and vegetables and in return they agree with us to take their children out of child labour and put them in school. A contract is drawn between us and the parents where the parent agrees that the child will not miss school and will no longer go to work. This is a fantastic way to both feed hungry children as well as ensure that they receive education.

SUSTAINABLE FOOD SOURCES
Planting trees, seeds, fruits and vegetables in poor villages in some of the countries mentioned above, the crop is then distributed equally between the poor villagers. We also build wells in Senegal, Iraq, Ethiopia, India and Liberia to provide children and families with clean drinking water.

Savoury

Sania's
Coconut-y Chicken and Sweetcorn Pasta

"I love making this with my mummy because it has sweetcorn in it (my favourite) and I get to pour in the coconut milk and help to shred the chicken and mix and mix and mix it all up very carefully with mummy by my side so I don't get burnt."

Feeds 5 pasta pals!

Recipe:

- 225g of uncooked pasta
- 1 tsp cumin seeds
- 1 1/2 tsp cumin powder
- 198g of canned sweetcorn
- 3 pieces of a medium sized chicken boiled with garlic, salt and pepper and shredded (left overs are great for this)
- 300-350ml of coconut milk
- Dash of lemon

1. Boil the pasta with salt and a tablespoon of oil and set aside.
2. In a pan heat a tablespoon of oil and add the cumin seeds and let them splutter then add the cumin powder and cook it slightly. Don't overcook this as burnt cumin tastes bitter.
3. Add your sweetcorn and cook.
4. Add coconut milk and salt and let it cook on low heat. Then add in the pasta and the chicken. A dash of lemon juice at the end just gives the dish that nice tang!

TASTY TIP: If you are cooking for grown-ups, you can add powdered chillies for that extra spicy flavour!

Husayn's
Chicken Roly Poly

"I love this mummum because it tastes so yummy, and I make the parathas with my mummy, then we roll it all up and turn it into a roly poly!"

Feeds 6 rumbly tummies

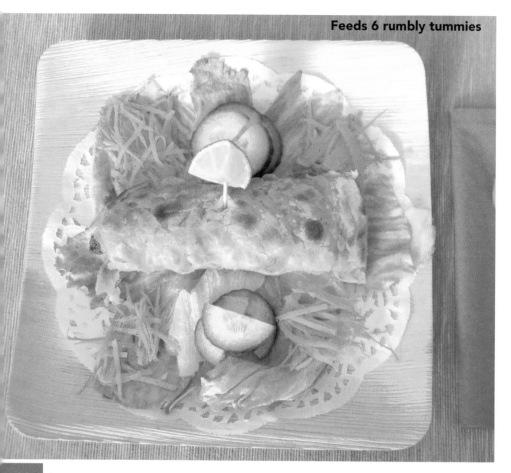

Recipe:

- 450g chicken breast cut into small pieces
- 1tsp garlic and ginger paste
- 1/2 tsp salt
- 1 tsp mint chutney
- 2 tsp tandoori masala
- 3 tsp tandoori paste
- 1 tsp lemon juice
- 1 tsp vinegar
- 2 tsp soya sauce
- 1 tsp paprika
- 5 tbsp yoghurt
- Fresh coriander leaves

For The Paratha:
- 250g plain flour
- 1 tbsp sugar
- 1 tsp salt
- 2 tbsp oil
- Warm water

1. To make the chicken filling, boil the ingredients together until there is very thick gravy.
2. For the paratha, combine the ingredients and form a dough using warm water.
3. For each paratha, Roll into a circle, add a few drops oil, spread it and sprinkle some flour, turn the circle into a fan, roll up into a circle and roll out like a roti. Cook with a little oil.
4. Once chicken ready put in the middle of cooked paratha, roll up and enjoy!

Hanna's
Fandabidosee Keema
and Mac Pie

"This is my favourite dish and I wish I could eat it all the time but my mummy makes it for me when I'm feeling poorly or it is a special occasion. I remember my Nani with a Sura al-Fatiha every time I have this as she used to make it for mummy when she was a little girl."

Feeds a family of 4

.Recipe:

- 500g dried cooked mince of your choice
- 2 large potatoes boiled, peeled and mashed to smooth consistency
- 600g boiled macaroni
- 200g grated mozzarella cheese
- 1 tbsp tomato purée
- Salt and pepper to taste

1. Preheat the oven to 200°C and lightly grease an ovenproof dish for your pie.
2. Add the tomato purée to the dried cooked mince and mix well.
3. Evenly distribute the cooked mince in the oven-proof dish.
4. Add the boiled macaroni on top of the mince layer evenly and sprinkle half of the cheese of cheese on top of this layer.
5. Now add the mashed potato as another layer of the pie and pat it down well with a flat spatula so it covers the other layer completely.
6. Sprinkle salt and pepper on the pie, cover with foil and place in the oven for 20 minutes. Reduce temperature to 180°C.
7. After 20 minutes take the pie out of the oven, remove the foil, add the remaining cheese and place in the oven for 5 minutes to melt or brown the cheese as desired.

TASTY TIP: *Serve your pie with a colourful salad, and enjoy your well balanced and delicious meal!*

Sarah & Mehvish's
Yummy Chicken Tikka Kababs

These chicken tikka kababs are our favourite. We love having it with either chips or plain white rice with butter; or even salad; hummm yummy...

Feeds 5 chicken chums!

Recipe:

- 450g chicken breast (cut into bite size pieces)
- 1 onion (cut into small slices)
- 2 peppers (cut into small slices)
- 1 tomato (diced; optional)
- 1 tsp salt
- 1/2 tsp black pepper
- Chilli flakes (adjust according to your taste)
- 1 tsp garlic paste
- 1/2 tsp coriander powder
- 1/4 tsp turmeric
- 250 ml yogurt
- 1/2 lemon (juiced)
- 1 1/2 tsp tandoori powder
- 1 tbsp oil
- Bamboo skewers

1. Mix all the ingredients together to form a paste and leave vegetables and chicken on side.
2. Coat the chicken and vegetables in the marinade and leave for at least 3 hours in refrigerator.
3. Preheat oven to 150°C. Grease a baking dish with few drops of olive oil and spread the marinaded chicken and vegetable pieces on it.
4. Bake for 10 minutes and flip the chicken pieces and again bake for 10 minutes.
5. Now take the baking dish out of the oven and place the chicken and vegetables on skewers (use paper towel to handle chicken if it is very hot). Place the skewers in the oven at 175°C for another 10 minutes (this gives the flavour and taste like tandoori). The yummy chicken tikka kabab is ready to be served!

Saniyya Zahra's
Yummy Buttered Makkai (sweetcorn)

"Butter corn is one quick snack that I love to prepare with my mummy. It is one of my favourite snacks; it will definitely be a hit if you make it for birthday parties or picnics."

Feeds 3 corn lovers!

Recipe:

- 3 sweetcorn cobs
- 1 tbsp butter
- Salt (to taste)
- Red chilli powder (to taste)
- 1 tsp black pepper powder
- Small bunch of finely chopped parsley

1. Boil some water in a large pot. Add salt and the corn cobs.
2. Cook for about 5 minutes. Remove the corn cobs and keep it in a kitchen towel to absorb the excess moisture.
3. Spread the butter on the corn. The warmth in the corn will melt the butter and help to spread easily.
4. Immediately sprinkle the chilli powder, pepper powder, little salt and finely chopped coriander around. It will stick to the butter. Put it on a skewer and enjoy the buttered corn on the cob.

TASTY TIP: After the corn is cooked you can peel the corn off the cob to a bowl using a sharp knife and serve the dish in a bowl! If you are in a hurry you can even use frozen corn (drain away excess water.) My mummy enjoys corn with chaat masala too!

Ammaar's
Favourite
Pirmohamed-Style Pilaw

"This is my absolutely favourite dish!"

Feeds 5 comfortingly!

Recipe:

- 500g lamb meat with bones cut into small pieces
- 3 onions (chopped)
- 1 tomato (chopped)
- 4-5 green chillies (crushed)
- 1 tbsp fresh garlic
- 1 tbsp fresh ginger
- Fresh parsley and coriander leaves chopped
- 4 large potatoes cut into 4 pieces each
- In a small plate have the dry whole Indian masala ready: (4 cloves, 5 cardamoms, 7 whole black peppercorns, 2 sticks of cinnamon, 2 tbsp cumin seeds and 2 bay leaves)
- 400g uncooked Basmati rice

1. Wash the meat with a bit of lemon juice and drain it. Boil the meat with garlic ginger paste, salt to taste and 3 cups of water until meat is cooked.
2. Soak the basmati rice in water for about 10 minutes.
3. In a large pan, heat 4 tablespoons of rapeseed oil and add the dry masala ingredients.
4. Once the whole masala begin to pop, add the chopped onions together with some freshly chopped parsley and mix on a medium heat until the onions become transparent. Add the freshly grated garlic and ginger.
5. Add the cut potatoes and stir well; then add the chopped tomatoes and mix well.
6. Add the boiled meat together with its broth and let it simmer for about 5 minutes.
7. Finally add the soaked rice and put about 3 flat tablespoons of salt. Add 2 cups of boiling water and Mix well and let it simmer on moderate heat. Cover the lid.
8. Once you see the rice is nearly cooked turn the heat on low and sprinkle some more freshly chopped coriander and parsley with the juice of one lemon and finally mix.
9. Cover the lid with foil paper and let the pilaw cook on very low heat for next half hour.

Ameera's
Appetizing Meat Pastries

"I love making pastries with my mummy! My favourite bits are: shredding the meat; mixing it with all the vegetables; rolling out the pastry and munching them of course!"

Feeds 8 (if you can have 2 each!)

Recipe:

- 1 kg boneless meat (boiled in ½ tsp salt, pepper, ginger and garlic paste)
- 3 tbsp spoon of oil
- 1 finely chopped onion
- 2 bunches of spring onions
- 2 green bell peppers
- 1 yellow bell pepper
- 5 green chillies
- Half a bunch of coriander crushed with a splash of lemon
- 1tsp garlic paste
- 1tsp ginger paste
- 2 tbsp tomato puree
- 1 tsp salt
- 1/2 tsp pepper
- 1/2 tsp garam masala
- 1/4 tsp turmeric
- 1tbs ketchup
- 1 egg
- 500g block of puff pastry

For the Filling

1. Marinade your meat with ½ tsp salt, ½ tsp pepper, ½ tsp ginger and ½ tsp garlic and boil.
2. Chop onions, spring onions and bell peppers into small cubes and stir-fry in hot oil.
3. Add garlic, ginger, salt, pepper, turmeric and stir.
4. Next, add tomato puree and ketchup to the mix. Add green chilli and coriander mix followed by garam masala. Simmer for a few minutes.
5. Finally shred the meat into the pot and mix.

For the Pastry

6. Preheat the oven to 200°C and slice pastry block into 16 equal squares (4 by 4).
7. Roll each square to an even thickness.
8. Fill the square with 1 heaped tablespoon of the meat filling.
9. Join two opposite corners of the square shaped pastry to form a triangular shape.
10. Press down edges to close the pastry and use a fork to create a shell-like pattern around the edges.
11. Beat an egg and lightly brush the pastries with it before placing them on a tray lined with baking paper in a pre-heated oven
12. Finally bake for approximately 15-20mins and enjoy!

Hayder's
Pakistani Kebab Burgers

"Mama, burger, burger, burger, dip"

Feeds 5 (with 2 each!)

Recipe:

- 450g beef mince (or you can use lamb)
- 1 medium onion
- 3 cloves garlic
- 2 green chillies
- A handful of coriander
- 3 tbsp gram flour
- 1 tbsp chilli powder
- 1/2 tbsp salt
- 1/2 tbsp ground garam masala
- Olive oil spray

To Serve:
- 10 Baps
- Cheese
- Red onions
- Ketchup/ chutney
- Cucumber
- Lettuce
- Tomatoes (or any other burger toppings)

1. Grind the onion, garlic, green chillies and coriander to make a paste and combine with the beef mince.
2. Add the chilli powder, garam masala, and salt to the mixture. Combine well.
3. Wet your hands with a bowl of warm water and take a ball of the beef mixture. Flatten it on your palm to make a burger shape.
4. Spray olive oil on a griddle pan and heat. Fry both sides of the burger for about a minute and half each side. Keep flipping the burger to cook both sides evenly.
5. Serve in a bap with your favourite burger toppings.

Hassan Zarringhalam's
Super Stir Fry

"I love to cook and this is one easy peasy recipe to make....everyone can make this it's really simple."

Feeds 4 stirfry superheroes!

Recipe:

- 1 onion (chopped)
- 2 peppers (chopped)
- 170g pack of noodles
- 1 big broccoli (cut into little florets)
- 135g baby corn
- 2 tbsp cooking oil
- 2 cloves garlic chopped
- 3 tbsp light soy sauce
- 1 tbsp sweet chilli

1. Sauté the onions in a pan with a little oil until they are translucent, then add the garlic.
2. Add the broccoli and peppers.
3. Once all cooked add the soy sauce and sweet chilli.
4. Stir all together.
5. Add in some cooked noodles.

Zahid's
Grab and Go Wrap

"This dish is so tempting, it is a roll of tasty, delicious goodness that will uplift your energy, and it is great before a game of football full of protein and carbohydrates."

Feeds 2 healthy helpers!

Recipe:

- 2 large free range eggs
- 1 tbsp olives (chopped)
- 1 tbsp mozzarella cheese (grated)
- 1 tbsp spring onions (chopped)
- 1 tsp green chillies (chopped)
- A pinch of salt and pepper
- 1 large tortilla wrap
- Spray oil

1. Crack the eggs into a plastic bowl, and whisk until well mixed.
2. Add chopped olives, grated mozzarella cheese, spring onions, green chillies, salt and pepper then set aside.
3. Heat a frying pan on medium heat, adding spray oil as needed.
4. Mix the egg mixture with a fork and pour into the frying pan.
5. Once omelette sets flip it over to cook the other side.
6. Heat tortilla wrap in the frying pan or microwave.
7. Place your cooked omelette on the heated tortilla. Roll it up and cut into half.

Maythams
Mouth-Watering Ondvo

"This is like an Indian cake and my best part is measuring everything for mummy and adding it to the mixing bowl. I love eating my Ondvo with Ambli (tamarind chutney)."

Feeds 16 (with a slice each!)

Recipe:

For The Batter
- 225g fine semolina
- 115g gram flour
- 1tsp garlic paste
- 1tsp ginger paste
- 4 tbsp yoghurt
- 4 tbsp oil
- ½ tsp citric acid powder or juice of half a lemon
- ¼ tsp turmeric powder; ¼ tsp chilli powder; 1 tsp salt
- 1 tsp dried yeast
- 220ml warm water
- ½ cup thinly chopped onion, ½ cup grated carrots, ½ cup thinly chopped cabbage. (We chop it all in the food processor because its much faster)
- 1 ½ tsp Eno fruit salt

Topping:
- 1tbsp oil
- 1tbsp sesame seeds
- 1tbsp black mustard seeds
- 1tsp curry leaves (limbro)
- ¼ tsp red dried chilli flakes

1. Mix all the ingredients for the batter except for the vegetables and Eno, and leave to rise for about 3 hours.
2. Preheat oven at 200°C.
3. Heat oil in a pan and add the sesame seeds, mustard seeds, curry leaves and chilli flakes. Let it sizzle until the aroma is released.
4. Add the chopped onions, cabbage and carrots into the batter. Add the Eno and mix until fluffy. Pour the batter into a well-oiled large cake tin. Pour the spices topping mixture evenly on top of your cake. Bake in the oven for about 20 minutes. Insert toothpick and the Ondvo is done if it comes out clean.

Ali's favourite
'Silver' Khichri

"I love eating khichri...everyday!!"

Feeds a family of 6

Recipe:

- 130g uncooked rice
- 130g split green moong lentils
- 850mls water
- 1 tbsp butter or ghee

- Rinse the rice and moong lentils thoroughly with cold water, drain them and place them into a saucepan.
- Pour the water into saucepan to cover rice and moongh lentils.
- Leave on medium heat to cook (being careful to watch that it doesn't boil over the pan).
- If the water dries up and the rice is not yet cooked keep adding more water a little at a time- it should be cooked within 20 mins.
- Once water has soaked up, add butter/ghee and mix well. The khichri will now be ready to serve!

TASTY TIP: I love to have milk with my khichri but other options include - kadhi, potato and aubergine curry...not forgetting the traditional poppadums!

Zahra's
Chachi's Easy Peasy Red Chicken

"My mummy learnt this recipe from a very special aunty and I really love it. I enjoy eating it with roast potatoes and parathas!"

Feeds 4 comfortably

Recipe:

- 500g boneless chicken (or you can use 1 baby chicken)
- 1 tbsp garlic and ginger paste
- 1 tbsp vinegar
- 4 tbsp soy sauce
- ¼ tsp chilli flakes / chilli powder (adjust to your taste)
- ½ tsp salt (adjust to your taste)
- 3 tbsp oil
- ¼ tsp turmeric powder
- 500g passata
- 1 tbsp fresh coriander (optional)

1. Wash the chicken and cut into medium sized cubes. Marinate with vinegar, garlic and ginger paste, soy sauce, salt and chilli flakes/powder. Cover, and set it aside for a minimum of 1 hour.
2. In a pan, heat the oil on a medium flame. Add the chicken and let it sizzle and brown. The liquid should have dried up.
3. To the leftover marinade, add the turmeric powder and the passata. Pour onto the chicken and cook for 5 minutes.
4. Lower the heat and cover to allow the chicken and tomato to cook properly. This should take about 10-20 minutes. It should become a thick maroon gravy.
5. Your dish is now ready! If you like, garnish it with coriander. (I don't like coriander so my mummy doesn't put it.)

TASTY TIP: Serve with yummy roasted potatoes and paratha with a fresh salad and enjoy!

Zahra's
Mouth-Watering "Maragi" in a Coconut Sauce

"My Naani makes this the best! I love the healthy beans and I like to eat it with rice – plain rice."

Feeds a family of 4

Recipe:

- 800g can of kidney beans (maragi)
- 400g chopped tomatoes
- 3-4 tbsp of coconut milk powder
- 1/2 tsp garlic
- 1/2 tsp salt, red chilli powder, turmeric
- 1 green chilli
- Coriander to garnish
- 1 tbsp oil

1. Chop the green chilli and add it to hot oil.
2. Blend the chopped tomatoes and add to pan.
3. Add garlic, salt, red chilli powder and turmeric and simmer.
4. Dissolve coconut milk powder in a mug with 3 tablespoons of boiling water and sieve into pot.
5. Drain kidney beans and add this to the coconut sauce.
6. Cook for 15-20 mins on a low heat.
7. Finally garnish with chopped coriander and enjoy!

TASTY TIP: This tastes even better when your grandmother feeds you! But you can also eat it with bread, chapatti or even mandazi!

Hussain Ali's
Scrumptious Stuffed Potatoes

"Why don't you try my stuffed potato recipe for a yummy way to make potatoes more fun!"

Feeds 4 potato pals!

Recipe:

- 4 large potatoes
- 1 tsp vegetable oil
- 1 tsp salt
- 200g cheese
- 200g sweetcorn
- 1 tsp butter

1. Preheat the oven to 200°C.
2. Rub the potatoes with oil and salt and put the potatoes in the oven for 1 hour.
3. Whilst the potatoes are in the oven, mix together the butter, sweetcorn, and cheese. Let the potatoes cool and then cut each potato lengthways.
4. Carefully scoop out the baked potato and fill it with the sweetcorn and cheese mixture.
5. Once you have filled the baked potatoes, place them in the oven for 15 minutes.

TASTY TIP: You can add any of your favourite vegetables, meats and cheeses to truly personalise the dish!

Zainab Zarringhalam's
Hummus Delight

"Hummus tastes creamy and nice! Not only is it healthy it goes with a lot of vegetables and is very good as a side dish!"

Feeds 4 delightful darlings!

Recipe:

- 200g canned chickpeas
- 2 tbsp lemon juice (adjust to taste)
- 2 garlic cloves (crushed)
- Salt to taste
- 100ml tahini (sesame seed paste)
- 2 tbsp extra virgin olive oil
- 1 tbsp plain yogurt

1. Drain the chickpeas and put in the food processor.
2. Add the lemon juice, garlic, salt, tahini, and yogurt in a food processor, and blend to a creamy purée.
3. Add more lemon juice, garlic, or salt to taste.
4. Turn out into a dinner plate and make smooth with the back of a spoon.
5. Drizzle with extra virgin olive oil.

TASTY TIP: Serve with hot pitta bread and lots of different vegetables like carrots, cucumber and peppers!

Sakinah & Haadi's
Favourite Roast Chicken

"We love it when mummy makes roast chicken for us!! Our favourite is when there are left overs for the next day! "

Feeds a family of 4

Recipe:

- 1 whole chicken (with or without skin according to preference)
- 2 vegetable stock cubes
- 2 tbsp butter
- 2 tbsp soy sauce
- Pinch of black pepper
- 4 onions

1. Wash the chicken and put into a roasting dish leaving it whole. Make slits in the chicken.
2. Melt the butter in the microwave or in a pan. Add the soy sauce, pepper, and stock cubes (simply crumble them in your hands and add). Mix this all together.
3. Pour this mixture over the chicken and rub it all over.
4. Cut the onions into quarters and stuff the chicken with them and put some around the chicken too.
5. Cover with foil and place in the oven at 180°C. Take out every 20 minutes to baste it.
6. Take out once the chicken is cooked through. It usually takes 70 minutes.

TASTY TIP: Enjoy this with our recipe for roasted new potatoes!

Maryam's
Sunday Roast Beef Sandwiches

"I love the taste of roast beef and cheese melting in my mouth."

Feeds 5 on a Sunday!

Recipe:

- 2 onions
- 450g beef
- 1 tsp garlic paste
- 1 tsp ginger paste
- 1 tbsp HP Sauce
- 1 tbsp Worcester sauce
- 1 tbsp soya sauce
- 1 tbsp American mustard
- 1 tbsp vinegar
- 1/2 tsp black pepper
- 1 tsp lemon

1. Fry the onions till they are golden brown in colour. Add the beef, garlic and ginger paste to the fried onion and cook the meat well.
2. Add the vinegar, soya sauce, HP sauce, Worcester sauce, mustard, black pepper and lemon. Mix these ingredients with the beef, and cook well.
3. Once the beef is tender, and has cooled down, shred the beef cubes.
4. Now for the Sandwiches: Spread mayonnaise or butter on sliced bread/baguette. Layer with lettuce leaves and finely sliced tomatoes. Spread the shredded beef evenly, and sprinkle grated cheese for extra flavor.

TASTY TIP: To make it even yummier, place the sandwiches in a sandwich maker (don't forget to butter the bread) and grill for a few minutes. Yum!

Yusuf's
Yummy Mini Pizzas

"I love making pizzas with my mummy and having loads of floury fun."

Feeds 4 mini munchkins

Recipe:

For the Base
- 225g strong white flour
- 1/2 tsp salt
- 2 tsp dry yeast
- 1 tsp vegetable oil
- 175ml warm water
- 2 tbsp flour for dusting

For The Topping
- 400g canned tomatoes
- 2 tbsp tomato puree
- 2 tsp dried oregano
- salt and pepper
- 150g cheese (I like cheddar cheese but you could also have mozzarella)
- Any other toppings (chicken, olives, pineapples, anything really!)
- 2 tsp olive oil

1. Mix the flour, salt and yeast in a bowl. Add the oil and water. Stir to make a soft dough.
2. Knead the dough on a floured surface for 5-7 minutes. Put it in a bowl, cover it with plastic wrap, and leave it in a warm place.
3. After about an hour when the dough has doubled in size, knead it again and divide it into 4 pieces.
4. Roll each piece into a circle and pinch up the edges of the dough. Grease the baking sheets. Place the bases on the sheets and leave them to rise while you make the topping.
5. Preheat the oven to 220°C. Drain the tomatoes and put it into a bowl with the puree and oregano. Mix and add salt and pepper.
6. Spread a quarter of the mixture on each pizza and arrange your toppings and cheese on top. Brush with olive oil, bake in the oven for 15-20mins and enjoy!

Ali Master's
"oh not so spicy" chicken noodles

"I love this recipe as it's very quick and yummilicious!"

Feeds 4 for lunch!

Recipe:

- 250g boneless chicken (cut into thin strips)
- ½ green pepper (cut into thin strips)
- 1 small onion (sliced)
- 4 small mushrooms (cut into thin slices)
- ¼ tsp salt
- ¼ tsp black pepper
- ½ tsp mixed spices
- 1 tsp chilli sauce
- 4 blocks of noodles
- 1 tbsp of oil

1. Marinate the chicken with mixed spices and the chilli sauce.
2. Prepare the vegetables by cutting them into thin strips.
3. In a wok, add the oil and stir fry the chicken for 5 minutes or until the chicken is tender.
4. Add the vegetables, salt and pepper. Stir fry for another 5 minutes.
5. In a separate pan, boil some water and add the noodles block. Boil for 4 minutes. Drain the water.
6. Add the boiled noodles in the wok with the chicken and vegetables. Stir fry for 1 minute. And serve hot.

TASTY TIP: Why not try using chopsticks?

Jawaad's
Chicken Corn
Soupelicious!

"I love this dish because it is the best soup in the world!"

Feeds 4 on a cold night!

Recipe:

- 500g boneless chicken (shredded)
- 1 tsp garlic paste
- 2 tsp olive oil
- ½ small onion (chopped)
- 220g tin of corn (roughly crushed-we use a blender)
- 3 tbsp cornflour (made into a smooth paste with 3 tablespoons on cold water)
- 1 egg (beaten)
- Water or chicken stock
- Salt (to taste)
- Pepper (to taste)
- Soya Sauce (to taste)

1. In a saucepan, heat the oil and add the onions. Stir until they become translucent. Add the garlic.
2. Add the shredded chicken and stir.
3. Add the crushed corn.
4. Add enough water or chicken stock to cover the mix and let it cook for 10 minutes on medium heat.
5. Add the corn flour paste and keep stirring until the soup is boiling. Then bring the heat down to a simmer.
6. Add beaten egg to the soup but keep stirring with a fork. (The egg should look like white strands in the soup).
7. Season to taste with salt, pepper and soya sauce.

TASTY TIP: Serve with garlic bread and enjoy!

Ammar's
Favourite Yellow Pasta

"I like to eat yellow pasta because it's yummy in my tummy"

Feeds 4 favourite friends!

Recipe:

- 400g uncooked pasta
- 1 onion (chopped into small pieces)
- 1 tbsp oil
- 2 carrots (chopped into cubes)
- 198g sweetcorn
- 400g kidney beans
- 10 green beans (cut into halves)
- 1/2 green pepper (cut into small pieces)
- 1/2 red pepper (cut into small pieces)
- 1/2 tsp salt
- 1/2 tsp turmeric
- 1/2 tsp garlic
- Coriander
- 300-350ml coconut milk

1. Boil the pasta in a saucepan and follow the next steps in another saucepan whilst pasta is cooking.
2. Sauté onion in oil until soft and transparent and then add salt, garlic and turmeric.
3. Add all the vegetables and mix well.
4. Let vegetables cook for about 4-5 mins on medium heat.

Grandkids
Garden Vegetable soup

"Nanny's soup will make you so strong!"

Feeds 4 great grandkids!

Recipe:

- 1 tsp oil
- 1 tsp plain flour
- 2 tomatoes (finely chopped)
- Vegetables (of your choice)
- 480ml water
- 2 tsp red lentils

1. Heat 1 teaspoon of oil and add the plain flour.
2. Stir and add the finely chopped tomatoes.
3. Cook for 5 minute and add any vegetables, we like peas, carrots, and corn.
4. Add the water and red lentils and salt and pepper to taste.
5. Let it simmer until vegetables are soft.

TASTY TIP: For a smooth textured soup, blend the soup mix, sprinkle with parsley and enjoy with a slice of fresh bread.

Hanna's
Cheesy Egg Muffins

"Cheesy Egg Muffins are my favourite for breakfast as a snack in the middle of the day, they are healthy and really tasty too!"

Feeds 6 (with 2 each!)

Recipe:

- 12 eggs
- 1/2 tsp sea salt
- Black pepper to taste
- non-stick cooking spray, to coat pans
- 225g spinach (frozen or fresh)
- 100g thinly sliced mushrooms
- 25g thinly sliced green onion
- 132g to 176g shredded cheese (either cheddar or parmesan)

1. Preheat the oven to Gas to 220°C. Crack eggs into a liquid measuring cup. Whisk the eggs and salt.
2. Grease a 12-cup muffin pan with oil. Divide spinach, mushrooms, green onion, and cheese between each muffin cup, then carefully pour eggs over tops until muffin tins are almost full (leave 1/4-inch space).
3. Bake for 20-25 minutes or until a toothpick inserted in the centre of a muffin comes out clean.
4. The egg muffins will look like a soufflé when they come out of the oven, but they will sink after a few minutes. Let them rest in the muffin tin for a few minutes before using a rubber spatula to carefully remove each muffin.

TASTY TIP: You can eat them straight away or let them cool and transfer to a re-sealable plastic bag. Refrigerate for up to a week or freeze for a month!

Haadi's
Roasted New Potatoes

"I love it when my mummy makes me freshly roasted potatoes with my dinner!"

Feeds a family of 4

Recipe:

- 1.5 kg new potatoes
- 2 tbsp Butter
- 1 tsp salt
- Pinch of black pepper
- 1 tsp mixed herbs

OR

- 1/4 - 1/2 tsp red chilli powder and 1/2 fresh lime

1. Wash and cut the potatoes in half and place them into an oven dish.
2. Melt 2 tablespoons of butter. Add 1/2-1 teaspoon of salt (to taste), a pinch of pepper, 1 teaspoon of mixed herbs (or 1/4 - ½ teaspoon of red chilli powder and juice of 1/2 a lime.)
3. Taste the mixture and add more seasoning accordingly. You should be able to taste the lime and chilli if using these.
4. Pour over the potatoes.
5. Bake in an oven uncovered at 190°C until the potatoes are cooked.

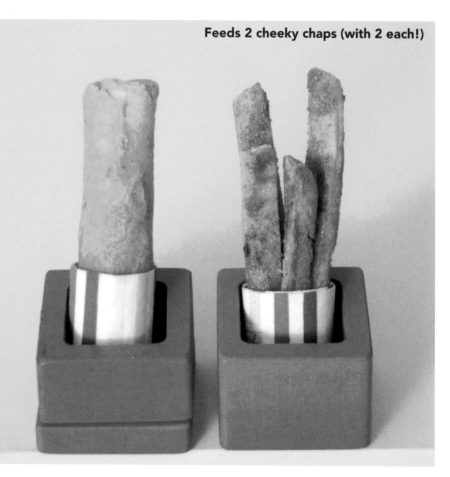

Hasan's
Cheeky Cheesy Roll Ups (and Cinnamon Crusts!)

"These cheesy roll ups are deeeelicious! They are cheeky because you even get dessert!"

Feeds 2 cheeky chaps (with 2 each!)

Recipe:

For The cheese roll ups
- 4 slices of bread
- 4 tbsp grated cheese, one tablespoon per slice of bread (we like mild cheddar, but you can use whichever cheese you like)
- 4 tsp butter

For the cinnamon crusts
- 1/5 tsp cinnamon
- 2 tsp sugar
- 2 tsp butter

1. Cut the crusts off the bread (keep aside for later) and using a rolling pin, roll the bread until it is about 3mm thick.
2. Sprinkle the cheese on each slice and roll it tightly.
3. Melt the butter in a shallow dish in the microwave, then dip each roll in the butter.
4. Sauté the rolls in a frying pan for 1-2 mins, continuously rotating so that they are evenly golden brown.
5. When you have eaten the rolls and it's time for dessert, melt the butter in a large bowl in the microwave and add the cinnamon and sugar. Mix well.
6. Put the bread crusts in the bowl and mix until they are evenly coated.
7. Sauté in a frying pan for 1-2 mins, turning continuously.

TASTY TIP: Enjoy the cheesy roll ups with a hearty bowl of tomato soup!

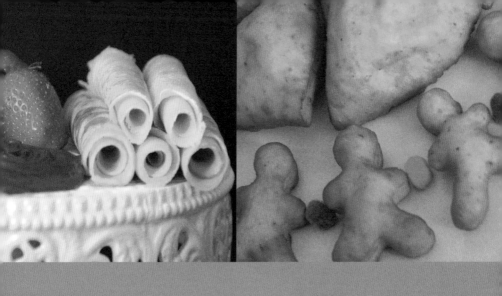

Sweet

Maa's
Ultimate Makate Siniya For The Mohameds

*"Although Maryam cannot speak properly just yet...
Actions speak louder than words! When there's makate
in the house, let's just say... It isn't there for very long!"*

Feeds 20 of Maa's mates!

Recipe:

- 450g rice (soaked overnight or at least for 3 hours)
- 300g sugar
- 1 block coconut cream bar (cut into pieces)
- 350ml warm milk
- 440ml warm water
- 2 tsp yeast (equivalent to 1 sachet)
- Cardamom powder (to taste)

1. Drain the water from the rice.
2. Put the rice in liquidiser (or blender).
3. Add coconut cream, water, milk and yeast.
4. Make sure it is liquidised into a very smooth liquid (must not contain any rice bits).
5. Pour the mixture into a suitable airtight container and place in a warm area to rise. This should take 3-4 hours.
6. Add sugar and cardamom (to taste) to the mixture and mix well.
7. Pre heat the grill on medium to high. Brush a non-stick frying pan with oil (can use any size, with this recipe we make 4 medium size makate (25cm diameter and 4cm thick), and heat on the stove. Once hot, lower the heat and pour the mixture into the frying pan. You will see bubbles and holes form in the makate.
8. Once the edges turn golden brown, place the frying pan under the grill to cook the top of the makate. Once it has turned golden brown, remove from grill.
9. Let the makate cool, cut into pieces.

Rahil and Zahid's
Thumbs Up Biscuits

"I love making these with my brother and my Mama, especially printing our thumbs and eating all the jam!! They are very yummy dipped in milk too."

Feeds 24 biscuit brothers

Recipe:

- 200g self-raising flour
- 100g caster sugar
- 100g butter
- 1 beaten egg
- 1 tsp vanilla essence
- 6 tbsp jam/marmalade/lemon curd or your choice

1. Preheat the oven to 190C°.
2. Rub the flour, sugar and butter together until the mixture resembles bread crumbs. Add the vanilla essence and the egg to from a dough.
3. Split the dough in half and then roll each half of the dough into a long tube shape.
4. Cut each of these tubes of dough into about 12 slices, each slices should be about 2cm thick and you should have about 24 slices in total.
5. Spread these slices on a large greased baking sheet. Keep some space between each one as they will spread whilst they are cooking.
6. Use your thumb to make a small indentation in each biscuit and fill the hollow with about 1/4 tsp of your jam.
7. Bake in the oven for 15 minutes until the biscuits are risen and golden brown; cool on a wire rack.

TASTY TIP: You can use different fillings such as marmalade, fruit jams and lemon curd to make the biscuits in all your favourite flavours.

Anum's
Squidgy Fruit Loaf

"I love eating apples and baking. My favourite thing is to mix the apples."

Feeds 4 fruity friends!

Recipe:

- 1 egg
- 3 tbsp of fruity fromage frais (I like strawberry)
- 1 1/2 tbsp caster sugar
- 135g self-raising flour
- 1/2 banana
- 1 gala apple
- 2 tbsp olive oil plus some extra for greasing the loaf tin

1. Preheat oven at 180°C.
2. Beat the egg and add the fromage frais. Whisk until well combined.
3. Add the flour, sugar and olive oil. Mix well.
4. Mash the banana with a fork and add to the loaf mixture.
5. Peel and chop the apple into bite size pieces. Add to the mixture and combine all the ingredients well.
6. Grease the loaf tin with olive oil and scrape the loaf mixture into the tin.
7. Bake for 25-30 mins or until golden brown. Let the loaf cool then decorate with fruit, slice the loaf and enjoy.

TASTY TIP: You can use any combination of fruit you like. Other favourites of mine are to add one chopped peach or raisins instead of the banana and apple.

Zahra's
Mini Oreo Cheesecakes

"I love making a mess when cooking with mummy."

Feeds 6 Oreo lovers!

Recipe:

- 17 Oreo cookies (standard size)
- 30g butter
- 170g cream cheese
- 85ml whipping cream
- ¼ tsp vanilla
- 4 tsp sugar
- 6 mini Oreos (to decorate)

1. Line a muffin tray with 6 large paper cases. Put the 12 Oreo cookies in a bag and crush them into crumbs using a rolling pin. Melt the butter and stir in the crumbs. Divide the crumbs between the muffin cases and press firmly into the base. Chill in the fridge whilst you prepare the filling.
2. Beat cream cheese, whipping cream, sugar and vanilla with an electric whisk in a large bowl.
3. Chop 4 of the Oreo cookies into tiny pieces and add to the mixture in the large bowl. Mix with a spoon until combined.
4. Spread the filling into the 6 muffin cases evenly. Chill in the fridge for at least 2 hours before serving.
5. Remove from the fridge and chop the remaining Oreo cookie into tiny pieces and sprinkle around the edges of each mini cheesecake.
6. Place a mini Oreo cookie in the centre of each cheesecake and enjoy!

TASTY TIP: *Using the same ingredients and method, you can make a single cheesecake for the whole famliy to share!*

Zaynab's
Hyderabadi Halwa Pooris

"Halwa pooris are one of my favourite dessert snacks to eat. I like putting the halwa filling in and sealing the poori. Sometimes my mom lets me eat them for breakfast too!"

Feeds 10 (one each!)

Recipe:

For Dough:
- 65g all-purpose flour
- 120g fine semolina powder
- 2 tbsp ghee
- 250ml warm Milk
- 1 pinch baking soda
- 1 pinch salt

For the Halwa Filling
- 60g of chana dal
- 1 tbsp almond powder (optional)
- 1/2 tbsp ghee
- 60g sugar
- 4 crushed cardamom seeds

- Oil for frying

1. In a large bowl, add flour, semolina powder, baking soda, and salt. Mix well and make a well in the centre.
2. Add the warm milk slowly, then knead thoroughly with your fingers until the mixture is combined.
3. Add the ghee then turn the dough onto the floured surface and knead until smooth and elastic. Then place the dough in a bowl and cover with plastic wrap and let it stand for 1/2 - 1 hour.
4. Add water and chana dal to a pot. Let it cook on medium heat for about 20 minutes until it is a tender paste.
5. In a non-stick saucepan, add ghee at medium heat. Once the ghee has melted add daal, almond powder, sugar, crushed cardamom, stir it well.
6. Now lightly flour the dough on the work surface and roll out palm sized circles. Add a heaped tablespoon of halwa mixture on one half of the circle dough.
7. Use a brush or your finger to put a little water around them. Fold it over, to make a half moon shape then press edges together with finger/fork to seal.
8. In a non-stick pan, add oil at medium heat. Then fry the poori. Let it fry both the sides until it is golden brown, about 3-5 minutes then remove from the heat, and drain on a kitchen paper.

Ali's
Yummy Crepes

"I make these crepes for breakfast and they are delicious and very easy to make."

Feeds 6 for breakfast!

Recipe:

- 70g plain flour
- 1 egg
- 100mls milk
- Pinch of salt
- Oil

1. Put the flour in a mixing bowl. Add the egg and a pinch of salt and mix it with a whisk.
2. While mixing, add the milk in small quantities until the batter is a smooth mixture.
3. Put a frying pan on medium/low heat. Add 1 teaspoon of oil and using a ladle put 1 ladle of the mixture into the frying pan. Ensure the mixture covers the whole of the frying pan to give a nice thin crepe.
4. Leave it for about a minute and then flip over. Again leave it for another minute.

TASTY TIP: Serve with topping of your choice. I love caster sugar and Nutella. Some of my friends like banana slices with chocolate sauce, maple syrup, honey. The choice is endless.

Muhammad
Master's Mandazi

"I love making mandazi as you get to play with flour. I also love rolling them and cutting them into different shapes. Best of all... I love eating them...yummy!"

Feeds 8 (if you can have 2 each!)

Recipe:

- 160g plain flour
- 80g self-raising flour
- 100g sugar
- 100ml coconut milk warm
- 1½ tsp of margarine
- 3.5g yeast
- ½ tsp of ground cardamom
- Oil for frying

1. Put the flour in a mixing bowl, add the margarine, sugar, yeast and cardamom. Mix it all well.
2. Add the coconut milk in small quantities and keep mixing it. Make into a soft dough and knead properly for at least 10 minutes.
3. Cover it with a cloth and leave it somewhere warm to rise. It can take up to 3 hours.
4. Gently knead again for 2-3 minutes.
5. Divide into 4 small balls. Roll it like a thick chapatti and cut it into 4 quarters.
6. Pour the oil in a small wok on medium heat. When the oil is hot, fry the mandazi 3 or 4 at a time, turn it with a slotted spoon until golden brown.
7. Remove it from the oil and place it on a plate with a kitchen towel.

TASTY TIP: Traditionally mandazi are triangular shaped but sometimes we use shape cutters like a ginger bread man or heart shape to make interesting shapes!

Amaanah's
Fun Flapjacks

"I love making flapjacks because they are yummy and healthy (come on they do contain oats!), and you can add berries, chocolate, raisins, coconut, nuts, or anything you wish- that's the fun bit!"

Feeds 10 fun friends!

Recipe:

- 500g porridge oats
- 250g butter
- 200g brown sugar
- 2-3 tbsp golden syrup (depending on how gooey you would like it)
- 227g desiccated coconut (optional)

1. Melt the butter in a saucepan on a low heat; whilst it's melting add the sugar.
2. Then add heaped tablespoons of golden syrup (if you want it less chewy, add less golden syrup).
3. When the sugar has dissolved, add the oats.
4. Add the desiccated coconut (optional). At this point you can add chocolate pieces or nuts.
5. Pour into a greased large dish or greased baking tray (25cmx25cm).
6. Bake on 190°C for 15-20 minutes.
7. Remove from the oven and let it set (it might be a bit gooey when you take it out).
8. When it is slightly warm score pieces with a pizza cutter. Only take them out when completely cooled.

Mahdiyya's
Delicious Banana Bread

"Banana Bread is my favourite weekend treat and I love it with a glass of cold milk!"

Feeds 10 banana buddies!

Recipe:

- 180g all-purpose flour
- 3-4 ripe bananas
- 40g melted butter
- 120g sugar (you can reduce to 90g for a less sweeter taste)
- 1 egg (lightly beaten)
- 1 tsp vanilla essence
- 1 tsp baking soda
- A pinch of salt

1. Pre-heat oven to 175°C.
2. Mash the bananas.
3. Using a wooden spoon, mix melted butter into the mashed bananas in a large mixing bowl.
4. Mix in sugar, egg and vanilla.
5. Sprinkle baking soda and salt over the mixture and stir them in.
6. Add flour last and mix until JUST incorporated. Do not over-mix.
7. Pour into buttered pan and bake for about 1 hour or until a toothpick inserted in the middle comes out clean.

Maryam Ali's
Vanilla Smoothie

"This smoothie recipe is amazing on a hot day!"

Fills a jug for 5

Recipe:

- 250g of mango
- 125ml of vanilla ice cream
- 4 strawberries
- 100ml of milk

1. Put the mango into your blender.
2. Add the strawberries and ice cream.
3. Add half of the milk and blend well.
4. After it's well blended, add the rest of the milk. Blend it till it's nice and smooth.

TASTY TIP: Try adding raspberries for an extra yummy touch!

Aliya and Hassan's
Fruity Oat Bars

"Scrumptious and delicious treat, perfect after school snack with milk or tea."

Feeds 21 (with 2 each!)

Recipe:

- 250g unsalted butter
- 300g brown sugar
- 150g honey
- 400g oats
- 300g dried fruits (we like cranberries, raisins and apricot)
- 300g seeds (we like sunflower and pumpkin seeds)

1. Put the butter, honey and sugar in a saucepan on low heat and stir until the sugar is completely dissolved.
2. Add the oats, dried fruit and most of the seeds (leave some to sprinkle over the top) – mix well.
3. Line a standard sized oven tray with baking paper and pour the mixture into the tray – press down and spread evenly.
4. Sprinkle the rest of the seeds over the top.
5. Drizzle an additional 2 tablespoons of honey over the top.
6. Bake for 30 mins at 160°C. Allow the mixture to cool completely before cutting to desired size.

Rayhan Ali's
Dairy Free Chocolate Cupcakes

"I love to make these cakes with my mummy because they taste so delicious."

Feeds **12 dairy free** dudes!

Recipe:

- 190g plain flour
- 128g sugar
- 1/2 tsp salt
- 1 tsp baking soda
- 3 tbsp cocoa powder
- 5 tbsp vegetable oil
- 1 tsp white vinegar
- 1 tsp vanilla
- 240ml water

1. Preheat oven to 175°C.
2. Mix all the dry ingredients together in a large bowl: flour, sugar, salt, baking soda, and cocoa powder.
3. Make three wells. Pour oil into one well, vinegar into the second and vanilla into the third.
4. Pour cold water over all and mix well with a fork.
5. Pour mixture into a cupcake tray and bake for 25-30 minutes or until tooth pick inserted comes out clean.

TASTY TIP: frost with your favourite icing.

Maryam's
Marvellous Marshmallow
Treats

"Marshmallows are one of my favourite things in the whole world – if I could I would eat these every day, for breakfast, lunch, and dinner!"

Feeds 12 marvellous mates!

Recipe:

- 50g unsalted butter
- 200g marshmallows
- 100g rice puffed cereal

1. In a large saucepan, melt the butter over a low heat.
2. Add the marshmallows and mix until they have completely melted. Remove from the heat.
3. Carefully mix in the cereal until it is completely coated.
4. Using some wax paper evenly press the mixture into 20x30cm tin. Cut into 5x5cm squares when cool.

TASTY TIP: I love to decorate these treats with icing and sugar pearls for special occasions - and if you are in a hurry, you can make this in the microwave!!

Ammaar's
Favourite Healthy Shake

"Healthy shakes are a great way to pack in a lot of nutrients! I find they give me lots of energy to do my homework straight after my after-school clubs!"

Fills 2 glasses with energy!

Recipe:

- 1 carrot
- 1 cucumber
- Few strawberries or raspberries
- Half a banana
- Few leaves of fresh spinach
- 1 tbsp fresh ginger
- 2 tbsp Greek Yoghurt
- 1 tbsp organic honey

1. Put all the ingredients in the blender or shake-maker and blend until smooth.

TASTY TIP: You can try any combination of ingredients –whatever is in the fridge! Sometimes for a treat, I also add a scoop of creamy vanilla ice cream!

Maysum's
Favourite Dessert
made by Nani

"Nani loves to make this for us (she makes nana use his muscles to stir it), and we love eating it just as much!"

Feeds a party of 20

Recipe:

- 175g semolina
- 227g butter
- 500ml whole milk
- 200g sugar
- 250g evaporated milk
- A few strands of saffron

1. Measure out the sugar, fresh and evaporated milk into a bowl and stir gently until all the sugar is dissolved. Add the saffron and stir. This is the liquid mixture.
2. Melt the butter in a deep saucepan on a high heat and carry on heating until all the butter has melted and the butter is warmed up and hot. Add the semolina to the warmed butter in the saucepan. Keep on high heat and stir vigorously until the mixture is bubbling and spitting.
3. Keep the mixture bubbling until the colour of the mixture is light golden brown (it takes two to three minutes from the time it started to bubble). Keep it on high heat.
4. Then, add the liquid mixture to the bubbling saucepan and keep on stirring all the time. The entire mixture will become a liquid. Keep stirring. The mixture will slowly warm up and become thicker and need more effort to stir. Keep on stirring vigorously. The mixture will thicken and will spit. Continue stirring until the whole mixture moves as one solid mass and the butter is released and you can see it on the sides of the saucepan. Stir for a minute more after that.
5. Switch off the heat, cover the saucepan and allow to stand. The siro is ready to serve.

TASTY TIP: Cover with crushed almonds and serve hot!

Mahdi's
Yummy Choco Treats

"This is my favourite 'treat' because I get to roll it into balls like playdough and cut out different shapes AND It's yummy so I can eat it too without mummy screaming 'Mahdi we don't eat playdough.'"

Feeds 10 (with a generous 3 pieces each!)

Recipe:

For the Chocolate Mixture
- 8 tbsp drinking chocolate
- 1 tbsp cocoa powder
- 10 tbsp icing sugar
- 9 tbsp milk powder
- A bit of milk

For the Coconut Mixture
- 16 tbsp dessicated coconut
- 5 tbsp icing sugar
- 6 tbsp milk powder

1. Use a few drops of milk to make each mixture into a play dough-like texture. You should have two balls, one chocolate, one coconut.
2. When the dough balls are ready grease your hands with a bit of butter and take some coconut mixture and mould it into small shapes with your hands or you can roll into balls and cut out shapes if you prefer and set aside.
3. Take some of the chocolate dough and flatten it out on your greased palm.
4. Place the shaped coconut mixture on it and close it over and press the ends together to seal it.

TASTY TIP: Make plenty - you can't just eat one of these mourish delights!

Husayn's
Healthy Pancakes

"Me like that!"

Feeds 1 little lad

Recipe:

- 2 medium eggs
- 1 medium to large ripe banana
- 3 tsp coconut oil (or oil of your choice)
- Toppings of your choice

1. Mash the banana with a fork until there are no lumps and fry in 1 teaspoon of coconut oil. Set aside.
2. Whisk the eggs and combine the eggs and banana.
3. Fry in 2 teaspoons of coconut oil until golden, turning once.

TASTY TIP: We like to add a sprinkle of cinnamon and sugar, but you could choose your favourite toppings. For example, raisins, desiccated coconut, or chopped nuts.

Hayder's
Healthy Apple and Sultana Muffins

"Like my sister, I love apples too. These treats are full of yummy apples and have no sugar (which is good according to my mum!)"

Feeds 12 at a party!

Recipe:

- 175g self-raising flour
- 100g sultanas
- 1/4 tsp cinnamon
- 1 tsp baking soda
- 2 apples
- 25g unsalted butter
- 2 tbsp honey
- 1 egg
- 50ml apple juice

1. Pre heat oven at 200°C.
2. Combine flour, baking soda, sultanas and cinnamon in a bowl.
3. Peel and grate the apples. Add the grated apples to the flour mixture and mix well.
4. In a separate bowl add the egg, butter, apple juice and honey. Beat well.
5. Combine the two mixtures together.
6. Line a cup muffin tray with muffin cases and pour the mixture evenly into the cases.
7. Bake for 15 minutes until golden brown.

Sanaa & Asad's
Treat Day Raw Chocolate Mousse

"Avocado - our favourite ingredient in the kitchen. This nice and smooth desert is mine and my little brother's favourite. A yummy chocolate treat that's got some healthy ingredients in them!"

Feeds 4 on treat day!

Recipe:

- 2 ripe avocados
- 175g medjool dates
- 45g raw cacao powder
- 120 ml milk of your choice (coconut/almond/soy milk)

1. Add the dates to food processor and process until the dates become a smooth paste.
2. Slowly add the remaining ingredients and process until smooth and creamy.
3. Leave the mousse in the fridge for at least an hour before serving.

TASTY TIP: Serve up in individual cups and top with raw cacao nibs, berries or walnuts for that extra special crunch!

NOTES

NOTES

NOTES